ST. MICHAEL
THE ARCHANGEL

". . . Michael, one of the chief
princes, came to help me . . ."
                    —Daniel 10:13

St. Michael casting Lucifer into Hell.

ST. MICHAEL THE ARCHANGEL

INCLUDING
PRAYERS TO ST. MICHAEL

"Quis ut Deus?"
"Who is like unto God?"

TAN BOOKS AND PUBLISHERS, INC.
Rockford, Illinois 61105

Nihil Obstat: William H. Baum, S.T.D.
               Censor Librorum

Imprimatur: ✠ Charles H. Helmsing
             Bishop of
                Kansas City-St. Joseph
             September 19, 1962

Originally published at Clyde, Missouri under the title
"'Neath St. Michael's Shield." 5th edition, 1962.

Retypeset and republished in 2006 by TAN Books
and Publishers, Inc.

ISBN 0-89555-844-0

Cover illustration and frontispiece: Photograph of
"Saint Michael the Archangel" stained-glass window.
Photo © 1992 Al Brown, Bardstown, Kentucky.

Printed and bound in the United States of America.

TAN BOOKS AND PUBLISHERS, INC.
P.O. Box 424
Rockford, Illinois 61105
2006

"AND THERE WAS a great battle in heaven, Michael and his angels fought with the dragon, and the dragon fought and his angels: and they prevailed not, neither was their place found any more in heaven, and that great dragon was cast out, that old serpent, who is called the devil and Satan, who seduceth the whole world; and he was cast unto the earth, and his angels were thrown down with him."

— *Apocalypse* 12:7-9

NOTE

In obedience to the decrees of Pope Urban VIII, no higher authority is claimed for what is related in this booklet than that which is due to human testimony, except insofar as the teaching of the Church is involved.

Contents

1. Devotion to St. Michael, Most
    Suitable for Our Times 1

2. Offices of St. Michael 4

3. Veneration of St. Michael 34

4. Prayers 41

ST. MICHAEL
THE ARCHANGEL

"But at that time shall Michael rise up,
the great prince, who standeth for the children of thy people: and a time shall come
such as never was from the time that nations
began even until that time. And at that time
shall thy people be saved, every one that shall
be found written in the book."

—Daniel 12:1

∽ *Chapter 1* ∽

Devotion
to St. Michael

Most Suitable for Our Times

LUCIFER has placed his stamp upon the present age. Open and secret revolt against God and His Church, the spirit of criticism, unbelief and immorality are spreading. The arrogant boast of Lucifer, "I will be like the Most High!" re-echoes everywhere. Puffed up with their discoveries and the progress in material science, men loudly proclaim their self-sufficiency and deny the existence of a Supreme Being. Governments and secret societies, plotting against God and striving to blot out from homes and schools, from offices and factories, all traces of Christianity, show plainly whose standard they follow. Never before in the world's history were God's rights so blasphemously mocked and denied, or the

1

rights of man so arrogantly asserted, as they are today.

These frightful evils must convince us that we must turn to St. Michael, the Archangel, that glorious prince of Heaven who rendered all glory to God, conquering Lucifer and casting him into the abyss.

Already three centuries ago, St. Francis de Sales wrote: "Veneration of St. Michael is the great remedy against despising the rights of God, against insubordination, skepticism and infidelity"—vices which are perhaps more prevalent now than ever before.

Surely, it is time for Christians to "rise from sleep" and to offer vigorous resistance to the enemies of salvation. The weapons in this conflict are not the arms of civil warfare, but the spiritual weapons of prayer and penance, increased fidelity to the Commandments of God, and frequent reception of the Sacraments. And surely we can choose no better leader in this conflict than the powerful captain who led the faithful Angels to victory.

Let us, then, with confident trust invoke the aid and the protection of this mighty Archangel whose shield bears the inscription: *"MI-CHA-EL"*—*"Quis ut Deus"*—"Who is like unto God?"

Chapter 2

Offices of
St. Michael

Prince of the Heavenly Hosts

THEOLOGIANS are of the opinion that St. Michael surpasses in glory and power all the other Angels in Heaven and possesses in the highest and most perfect degree the zeal and the love peculiar to the highest Seraphim. The title *Archangel* does not, in accord with the words of St. Peter and St. Jude Thaddeus, signify that St. Michael belongs to the choir of angels designated by that name, but that he is an angel of *superior rank*. The Church also invokes him as the *prince* of the Angels, who has supreme command over all the heavenly hierarchies.

This position of honor was merited by St. Michael in the battle which he waged against Lucifer and the rebellious angels before the creation of the world. When God created the Angels as magnificent spirits of light and love, which in countless hosts surround His heavenly throne, He bestowed upon them most eminent gifts of nature and grace. But before admitting them to the unveiled vision of His glory in Heaven, He placed them under probation, just as later He subjected mankind to a trial of obedience in the persons of Adam and Eve. The nature of the trial is not known with certainty. Learned and saintly theologians hold that the Heavenly Father revealed to the Angels the future Incarnation of His Divine Son, whom they were to adore in His Sacred Humanity. At the same time He revealed to them the surpassing dignity and glory of Mary, whom, as the Mother of God, they were to venerate as their Queen.

Lucifer, one of the most glorious and exalted princes of the heavenly court, dazzled by the splendor of his own gifts, rebelled at the thought that human nature should be preferred to his own angelic nature. He would not acknowledge that a woman, inferior to him in nature, should at some future time be made his Queen, and that the seed of that woman should be preferred to himself for the honor of the hypostatic union. Desiring for himself the prerogatives of the God-man, he raised his great battle-cry of rebellion: "I will be like the Most High!" (*Is.* 14:14).

Some have held that, in their pride, a third of the angels took up Lucifer's rebellious cry. At the same instant another great Archangel, equal in beauty and grace to the proud Lucifer, prostrated himself before the throne of God. With an act of profound adoration, he opposed the cry of the rebellious angels with his own battle-cry of love and loyalty: *"Mi-cha-el"*—"Who is like unto God?"

The fearlessness and fidelity of this mighty champion roused the faithful Angels, who rallied to his standard, repeating with one accord: "Who is like unto God?" Then followed that tremendous battle between the good and the bad angels which St. John describes in the *Apocalypse*: "And there was a great battle in heaven, Michael and his angels fought with the dragon, and the dragon fought and his angels: And they prevailed not, neither was their place found any more in heaven. And that great dragon was cast out, that old serpent, who is called the devil and Satan, who seduceth the whole world." (*Apoc.* 12:7-9).

Thus, St. Michael and his faithful followers won a glorious victory. With the swiftness of lightning, Lucifer and his companions were transformed into hideous demons and cast into the abyss of eternal torment and darkness, which God created for them. In reward for his zeal and fidelity, the holy Archangel Michael was made prince and commander-in-chief of all the heavenly legions. The Angels most willingly and gratefully recognize his supremacy, for after God, they owe to him their perseverance in grace and their eternal happiness. With loving submission they receive from him their various offices. They are attentive to his slightest wish, seeing in his commands and regulations the will of God, the sovereign Lord and King of all. Thus St. Michael receives highest honor among the Angels in the heavenly court.

On our part, also, he deserves highest honor among the Angels. Since he was the first to recognize and adore the Word-made-flesh, and the first to be illumined by His grace, he is the "first Christian." He is also the "first Apostle," because he was the first to announce the Saviour to the angelic choirs. He is the "first lieutenant" of Jesus Christ, for he was the first to lead the faithful servants of God to victory against the enemy.

Defender of God's People in the Old Testament

Both in the Old and the New Testament, the holy Archangel Michael is called the *guardian angel of the people of God*. He is also honored as the *Herald of the General Judgment* and the *Guardian of Paradise*. It is his office to lead all the elect into the Kingdom of Eternal Glory.

The world's history is replete with instances of St. Michael's solicitude for the children of men during the time of their earthly pilgrimage. He began to fulfill his office as defender and leader of God's people in the Garden of Paradise. St. Ambrose says that God commissioned St. Michael to lead Adam into Paradise, to explain to him the purpose of his creation, to guide him and to associate with him in visible form. After the fall of Adam and Eve, this same glorious Archangel stood guard at the gate of Paradise with flaming sword, "to keep the way of the tree of life." (*Gen.* 3:24).

The Fathers of the Church tell us that even though in many instances the name of St. Michael is not mentioned in Holy Scripture, when reference is made to the services of an angel, we may confidently believe that it was either St. Michael himself who rendered assistance, or his angelic subjects, who did so at his command.

They speculate that it may have been St. Michael who warned Noe of the coming flood, and that it was through St. Michael that Abraham was named the father of the chosen people and received that wonderful promise which Holy Church has immortalized in her prayers for the dead: "May the holy standard-bearer, Michael, introduce them into that holy light which Thou didst promise of old to Abraham and his descendants." The Angel who appeared to Moses in the burning bush (*Ex.* 3:2) was St. Michael, according to the teaching of St. Gregory Nazianzen. It was this mighty Angel who performed the wonders which took place at the departure of the Israelites from Egypt, and through whom God gave the Ten Commandments to the Israelites on Mount Sinai. Likewise, the Angel who routed the army of Sennacherib (*4 Kings*

19:35) was the holy Archangel Michael.

After the death of Moses, according to an ancient Jewish tradition to which St. Jude refers in his Epistle (*Jude* 1:9), St. Michael concealed the tomb of Moses from the people, and also from Satan, who wished to disclose it to the Israelites to seduce them thereby to the sin of false worship.

God revealed to St. Michael the designs of His justice and mercy regarding His chosen people. Of this the prophecies of Daniel and Zacharias bear witness. Finally, it was this great celestial prince who aided the Israelites and rendered the army of Judas Macchabeus victorious over their enemies.

(Even to this day the Jews invoke the holy Archangel Michael as the principal defender of the Synagogue and their protector against enemies. On the Feast of the Atonement they conclude their prayers with this beautiful invocation: "Michael, Prince of Mercy, pray for Israel, that it may reign in Heaven, in that light which streams forth from the face of the King who sits upon the throne of mercy.")

Protector of the Church

Just as the chosen people of the Old Law

were marvelously protected by St. Michael, so we may believe that this same prince of Heaven protects the Church of God even more wonderfully. Under the New Law, as under the Old, St. Michael is the "Vicar of the Most High and the Prince of His people," ever prepared to render assistance. The Fathers of the Church are of one mind in teaching that *St. Michael is the guardian angel and the protector of the Catholic Church.*

Time and again, in centuries past, St. Michael came to the rescue when dreadful wars and persecutions threatened to destroy Christianity. He it was who, at the command of Mary, Queen of Angels, came to the assistance of Constantine the Great in the fourth century and helped his forces to gain a brilliant victory over the pagan Emperor Maxentius. The Archangel himself revealed his identity in this instance. Appearing to Constantine after the completion of a beautiful church, which the latter had erected to his honor in gratitude, he said: "I am Michael, the chief of the angelic legions of the Lord of hosts, the protector of the Christian Religion, who while you were battling against godless tyrants, placed the weapons in your hands." This famous edifice, generally known as the *Michaelion*, has been the scene of many miracles wrought through the great Archangel.

Later, St. Michael proved himself a powerful protector against the invasions of barbarian hordes. The Greek Emperor Justinian I erected six churches in his honor, in grateful recognition of this assistance. St. Joan of Arc, the Maid of Orleans, who in the fifteenth century saved France, ascribed her vocation and her victories to St. Michael. Three times he appeared to her and informed her that she was called to deliver her country. In the sixteenth century, when it seemed that the Turks (Muslims fighting under the Turkish sultan) would conquer all Europe, St. Michael at the command of the Blessed Virgin again championed the cause of the Christian (Catholic) Faith, and a glorious victory was gained over the infidels at the Battle of Lepanto in 1571.

Thus has St. Michael proved himself a valiant warrior for the honor of God, both in Heaven and on earth. And he still wages incessant war with the archfiend Satan in the great Kingdom of God upon earth, the Church.

Blessed Anne Catherine Emmerich was reputed to have had visions of the past and future combats of the Church. Repeatedly she saw St. Michael, in the form of a warrior, standing above the Church, replacing his blood-stained sword in its scabbard as a sign of victory. She was also shown how, in the present-day struggles of the Church, St. Michael would bring about a most glorious victory. This thought should be consoling to all faithful Christians who view with alarm the many shafts of persecution now being directed against the Church.

Pope Leo XIII, realizing by divine enlightenment the present and future struggles of the Church against the powers of Hell, felt convinced that through the intervention of St. Michael, Hell would be conquered and the Church restored to peace and liberty. He therefore composed a prayer in honor of this warrior Archangel and ordered it to be recited daily after low Mass in all the churches throughout the Christian world. (See page 45.)

It is said that one day, having celebrated the Holy Sacrifice, the aged Pontiff was in conference with the Cardinals. Suddenly, he sank to the floor in a deep swoon. Physicians who hastened to his side feared that he had already expired, for they could find no trace of his pulse. However, after a short interval the Holy Father rallied and, opening his eyes, exclaimed with great emotion: "Oh, what a horrible picture I was permitted to see!" He had been shown in spirit the tremendous activities of the evil spirits and their ravings against the Church. But in the midst of this vision of horror, he had also beheld consoling visions of the glorious Archangel Michael, who had appeared and cast Satan and his legions back into the abyss of Hell. Soon afterward, he composed the well-known prayer: "St. Michael, the Archangel, defend us in the battle. Be our defense against the wickedness and snares of the devil. . . ."

The Church has special need of St. Michael's powerful protection in our times. On all sides she is assailed by strong and bitter enemies. In one country after another, religious persecution rises to an ever higher pitch of hatred and insolence. The terrible crimes which have been committed in recent times, and are still being committed against the Church, both in her sanctuaries and against her members, surely are instigated by the devil. No human mind could be base enough to conceive and put them into execution.

We know that the gates of Hell shall never prevail against the Church, for Our Lord has promised to be with her till the End of Time, but we must do our part in defending her cause. God might have cast the rebel angels down into Hell by a single act of His Will, but He chose rather to send against them His armies of loyal spirits under the leadership of the great St. Michael. So too, in the present critical times, He could confound the enemies of the Church by merely willing to do so. But He wills, rather, that we should cooperate in her defense under the leadership of the Great Captain of the heavenly hosts.

Helper and Defender of Christians

Besides the protection which the glorious Archangel Michael extends to the Church at large, he is also the protector of every individual Christian and of all Christian nations. How fortunate we are in having so powerful an advocate! Surely, never so urgently as at the present time have

Catholics needed St. Michael's help to
remain steadfast in their Faith. Unbelief
has carried its insolence to the very limit
and boldly proclaims that there is no God.
Blasphemy against Jesus Christ, against
His mysteries and His doctrines has
increased in the most frightful manner. It
is our duty to be faithful Catholics, to con-
fess our Faith openly and energetically and
to preserve a glowing, invincible love for
Jesus Christ.

St. Michael is the conqueror of Satan.
Under his leadership, let us unfurl everywhere the banner of the Catholic Faith and
have no fear of godlessness. In a thousand
secret ways, Satan plots and wars against
God and tries to usurp His throne. Let us
keep the kingdom of our heart firmly closed
against him, that he may never reign
therein by sin. When the spirit of darkness
incites us to thoughts of pride or rebellion,
let us answer him with St. Michael: "*Who
is like unto God?*" Who am I—a creature of
dust and ashes, the fleeting phantom of an
hour—in comparison to God? When Satan
tries to seduce us to commit this or that
sin; when in alluring pictures he presents
to us the pleasures and attractions of this

world; when he promises us honors, riches, happiness, on condition that we break a Commandment, omit a good work, or commit an evil deed; when he tempts us to give way to murmuring and impatience and to find fault with the inscrutable ways of Divine Providence; when the siren song of sinful pleasures sounds in our ears, filling our hearts with unholy longings and crowding our imagination with forbidden sights and scenes; then let us ever oppose the tempter with the same energetic words: *"Who is like unto God?"*

"Our whole life," says St. Bernard, "is a continuous temptation." He drew this truth from Holy Scripture. We have to battle against foes who are mighty in power, cruel in their vengefulness, fearsome in their craftiness, countless in their number, tireless in their persecutions. They are spirits who deal blows without being seen, who intrude everywhere, who see everything that we do, while remaining invisible to us. And they battle with weak persons who wander in darkness, on slippery paths, surrounded by frightful abysses. With furious rage these many enemies have sworn to avenge themselves upon us, because God

has called us to occupy the thrones left
vacant by them. They are bent upon the
eternal ruin of our *souls*.

The number of the demons is incredible.
St. Anthony of the Desert (251-356) said
repeatedly that *millions* of evil spirits were
roaming about the world. And the influence
which these evil spirits exercise over world
events is tremendous. Yet we need not
despair, because St. Michael is a defender
more powerful by far than the spirits of
darkness. In the prayer of the Church we
daily ask him to "cast into Hell Satan and
the other evil spirits, who prowl about the
world seeking the ruin of souls."

Viewing the world situation in the spirit
of faith, we cannot deny that the great evils
which now afflict the world will never be
amended without *prayer* and *penance*. Yet
even Catholics have lost sight of this truth.
They pray for the cure of the sick, for suc-
cess in their undertakings and for many
other personal intentions—but not enough,
or not at all, *for the cessation of the pre-
vailing moral evils* which mean triumph for
Satan and ruin for the Church and for
souls. The beautiful prayer given on page
57, also propagated by Pope Leo XIII (1878-

1903), deserves to be taken to the hearts of all Catholics and recited by them frequently, and even daily. It is a prayer peculiarly applicable to our times and to all Christendom.

The life of St. Oringa (d. 1310) records an incident of protection by St. Michael, the Archangel: One day the Saint, in company with several other young women, started on a pilgrimage in honor of St. Michael to Monte Gargano, in Italy. The journey extended over a number of days. On the way, the little company was joined by a few men who feigned to be pilgrims and excellent guides. The men seemed to be very pious, and they cunningly kept up an edifying conversation until evening. In reality, they were robbers in disguise, who had evil designs regarding the virgins. They led them directly to their den. Suddenly, a youth of heavenly beauty appeared to the maidens, calling out in a powerful voice: "Flee from here! Your souls are in danger!"

For a moment, the robbers were paralyzed with terror. In the meantime, the noble youth guided the maidens to a safe lodging some distance from the den. Later, it was revealed to St. Oringa that this rescuer was none other than St. Michael the Archangel.

Heavenly Physician

In the early ages of the Church, devotion to St. Michael was very popular. The early Christians invoked him especially for the cure of the sick. Tradition relates that in the earliest ages, St. Michael caused a medicinal spring to spout at Chairotopa near Colossae, and that all the sick who bathed there, invoking the Blessed Trinity and St. Michael, were cured. Still more famous are the springs which St. Michael is said to have drawn from the rock at Colossae itself. The pagans directed a stream against the sanctuary of St. Michael to destroy it, but the Archangel split the rock by lightning to give a new bed to the stream and sanctified forever the waters which came from the gorge.

At Constantinople, likewise, St. Michael was the great heavenly physician. The Christians of Egypt placed their life-giving river, the Nile, under the protection of St. Michael.

In Rome, also, the role of heavenly physician was assigned to St. Michael. During the pontificate of St. Gregory the Great (590-604), a terrible pestilence depopulated the city of Rome. The Sovereign Pontiff ordered a penitential procession, during which he himself carried a statue of the Blessed Virgin. Eighty persons died in the ranks of the procession itself. Still the Pope continued the prayers. When they arrived at the bridge crossing the Tiber, they heard the song of angels in the skies. Suddenly, above the castle of St. Angelo, St. Michael appeared in gigantic size. In his right hand he held a sword which he thrust into the scabbard. At the same moment the pestilence ceased.

The celebrated sanctuary of Mont Saint-Michel in Normandy, France, has likewise been the scene of many marvelous cures, wrought through the intercession of the great Archangel. During the middle ages, this mount was one of Europe's most renowned places of pilgrimage. This sanctuary owes its origin to an apparition of St. Michael to St. Aubert, Bishop of Avranches, during the eighth century. Appearing to the holy Bishop, the Archangel pointed out to him a tall cliff extending out into the sea, telling him that this spot was under his special protection and requesting that a church be built there in his honor. An imposing church was erected on the rocky mount, at the cost of great hardships and difficulties. Here the glorious Archangel testified to the truth of the apparition by effecting many and wonderful cures. Twelve blind persons had their sight restored, and many sick were cured of their diseases. From that time forward, the Archangel Michael has been highly venerated throughout France.

Up to the time of Charles XI (1848-1903), every Frankish king made a pilgrimage to this mount. Here Charlemagne dedicated his mighty kingdom to the Archangel. This church, with a Benedictine monastery adjoining, has a view far out over the sea. Its many steeples give it the appearance of a fortress. During the French Revolution, the monastery was converted into a central prison, and pilgrimages ceased. During the past few decades, however, the veneration of St. Michael at this sanctuary has been given a new impetus, and large pilgrimages are once more ascending the holy mount to honor God through His glorious Archangel.

From the history of Mont Saint-Michel and Monte Gargano (see p. 35), it is evident that pilgrimages are pleasing to the great Archangel and that special graces are obtained in this manner. However, since few persons are in a position to make pilgrimages to such celebrated shrines, one may instead visit any church or chapel, or even venerate a picture of the Archangel. If such visits are repeated several times, or even *nine times* as a *novena*, and are united with assistance at Holy Mass and the reception of Holy Communion, one may trustfully expect the aid of the holy Archangel, even in the gravest necessities.

Advocate of the Dying

Not only during life does the glorious Archangel Michael defend and protect souls, but he is their special advocate and consoler at the hour of death. When the last hour of our earthly career draws near and we are confronted by that awful moment when our soul must leave the body, which it has loved so much, satanic hosts, like ravenous lions, will make a last attack upon us. But we need not fear if during life we have been faithful in venerating St. Michael and in imploring his aid for the hour of death. In that hour of supreme need, this invincible Archangel, ever ready to assist the faithful soul, will come to our aid with his hosts and do battle on our behalf. He will cover us with his strong shield and lead us safely through the midst of our enemies.

And when at length our souls have been freed from their earthly bonds, he will conduct us to the judgment seat of Christ, where he will undertake our defense and implore the forgiveness of our sins. Finally, if we have merited to be numbered among the elect, he will take us beneath his glorious banner and conduct us to the blessed home of light, where all the Angels and elect children of God glory in the eternal praise of their Creator. It is therefore a commendable practice daily to invoke St. Michael to lend his assistance at the critical hour of death. Many are the faithful clients of St. Michael who have experienced his help in that hour.

Among the writings of St. Alphonsus Liguori, we find the following account of St. Michael's assistance at the hour of death. A certain Polish gentleman had for many years led a wicked life. When the hour of death approached, he was filled with terror and tortured by remorse of conscience over his former recklessness, so that he was reduced to a state of utter despair. No amount of exhortation or encouragement had any effect upon him; he refused every spiritual consolation.

This unhappy man, however, still had some veneration for St. Michael, and God in His mercy permitted the holy Archangel to appear to him in his last struggle. St. Michael encouraged him to repentance and said that he had prayed and obtained for him sufficient time to regulate the affairs of his soul. Shortly afterwards, two Dominican priests came to the house, saying that a stranger had sent them. The sick man recognized this as the work of St. Michael. He confessed his sins amid tears of repentance, received Holy Communion with touching devotion, and breathed forth his soul with every indication of being truly reconciled with God.

Consoler of the Poor Souls

In her beautiful prayers in the Mass for the Dead, the Church with maternal solicitude places the souls of her departed children in the hands of St. Michael, that he may lead them into the kingdom of everlasting light. If St. Michael is so solicitous for the welfare of souls during their lifetime and at the hour of death, we may be certain that he will also befriend them during their stay in Purgatory and will hasten to bring them consolation.

A Cistercian monk appeared to a priest friend soon after his death and told him he would be delivered from Purgatory if during Holy Mass the priest would recommend his soul to St. Michael. The priest complied with this desire, and he, together with others who were present, had the consolation of seeing the soul of his friend taken to Heaven by the Archangel.

It is related that a certain priest, one day while offering the Holy Sacrifice for the dead, recommended some souls in a particular manner when pronouncing the words: "May the Prince of the Angels, St. Michael, lead them into the glory of Heaven." At the same time he saw the glorious Archangel descend from Heaven into Purgatory to deliver those souls and to conduct them into Paradise.

Let us be encouraged by these examples to invoke St. Michael frequently on behalf of our departed loved ones, and in particular to recommend them to his powerful intercession during the celebration of Holy Mass.

"The Prince of the heavenly militia," says St. Anselm, "is all-powerful in Purgatory, and he can assist the Poor Souls whom the justice and sanctity of the Almighty retain in this place of punishment." "It is incontestably recognized since the foundation of Christianity," declares St. Robert Bellarmine, "that the souls of the Faithful departed are delivered from Purgatory through the intercession of St. Michael the Archangel." Let us add to these authorities the words of St. Alphonsus Liguori: "St. Michael has received the care of consoling and helping the souls in Purgatory."

Guardian of the Blessed Sacrament and of the Pope

When the Second Person of the Blessed Trinity became man, the sublime office of guarding the Saviour during the thirty-three years of His earthly life fell to God's zealous advocate, St. Michael. This is the pious belief of eminent Doctors and theologians. And since the Ark of the Covenant has been replaced by the Tabernacle, St. Michael guards the Blessed Eucharist and keeps watch over the thousands of tabernacles and altars scattered throughout the world. Even so, he zealously guards and protects Christ's Vicar upon earth, the reigning Pope.

It has been revealed to various Saints that the great Archangel is the special guardian of the Blessed Sacrament; that he accompanies it everywhere: in the hands of the priest, upon the throne of exposition, in the tabernacle, when borne in procession, on its obscure visits to the sick, or wherever the love of the Divine Victim may cause it to be borne. Day and night, he keeps faithful vigil before the tabernacle in loving adoration.

At the beginning of Holy Mass, his name is mentioned in the confession of faults made by the priest at the foot of the altar, and by the faithful in turn. At the Offertory of a Solemn High Mass the priest implores the blessing of the Almighty upon the oblation, *through the intercession of St. Michael*. And during the Canon of the Mass, after the Consecration, the priest prays God to command that the oblation be borne by the hands of His holy angel to His altar on high. The Angel here referred to is doubtless the Archangel Michael. With loving solicitude, he watches over all the tiny particles which fall from the consecrated Hosts at the time of Holy Communion, that they may not be lost or desecrated.

The liturgy also presents St. Michael to us as the incense-bearer standing beside the altar as our intercessor and as the bearer of the Church's prayers before the throne of God. "An angel stood near the altar of the Temple, having a golden censer in his hand, and there was given to him much incense; and the smoke of the perfumes ascended before God." (*Offertory, Mass of St. Michael*).

Christ silent and veiled in the Holy Eucharist and Christ visible and speaking to us in the person of the Pope—these are the two objects of Satan's inveterate hatred and rage. And these are also the two objects of St. Michael's greatest devotion and solicitude. Let us range ourselves under the banner of St. Michael, and by active zeal in the interests of Jesus, atone for the many outrages against the Blessed Sacrament and Christ's Vicar.

A Miraculous Rescue

In York, England, during the reign of the monarch Charles II (1660-1685), some ruffians gained entrance to the convent of St. Mary and, amid curses and blasphemies, were making their way toward the chapel to outrage the Holy Eucharist.

The superioress of the convent had obtained permission, in case of extreme danger, to carry the Blessed Sacrament to safety. As the furious mob pressed into the convent, she hastened with her Sisters to the chapel. With trembling hands and reverential awe, she opened the tabernacle, grasped the ciborium, concealed it beneath her flowing mantle and turned to flee. But at that moment the persecutors pressed into the corridor leading to the chapel and cut off all means of escape. After a moment's reflection, the superioress commanded the Sisters to place the statue of St. Michael before the door of the chapel. At the same time, she cried out with a loud voice: "Great God, protect Thyself, for we are no longer able to rescue Thee!"

The cursing, raging mob had already reached the open door of the chapel when suddenly, in an inexplicable manner, the men shrank back, astounded and stupefied before the statue of St. Michael. In a few moments not a single one of the intruders remained in the convent.

In thanksgiving for this miraculous rescue, the statue of St. Michael was erected permanently at the entrance of the chapel and the feast of the Archangel was celebrated each year with great solemnity.

At the End of Time

The thought of the Day of Judgment justly fills every thinking soul with a wholesome fear. God has mercifully concealed from us the day and the hour when this dread event shall occur. Our Lord Himself, after describing the terrors of the End of the World, said to His disciples: "But that day and hour no one knoweth, no, not even the angels of heaven, but the Father only." (*Matt.* 24:36). Nevertheless, Our Lord foretold certain signs which would precede the End of the World and be a warning of its approach. These signs are described in the 24th chapter of the Gospel of St. Matthew.

When the End of the World draws near, St. Michael will wage a final battle against the Antichrist, who by false miracles will endeavor to seduce even the elect of God. St. Michael will then defend the Church against frightful persecutions. This is foretold in the Book of Daniel, where the prophet, speaking of the End of the World and the Antichrist, says: "At that time shall Michael rise up, the great prince, who standeth for the children of thy people. And a time shall come such as never was, from the time that nations began even until that time." (*Dan.* 12:1).

After this most valiant Archangel has once more conquered the Prince of darkness and has cast him into the abyss of Hell, he will sound the dread trumpet, whose resonance will call the dead to life and summon all men before the Eternal Judge to receive their final sentence of reward or punishment. Happy shall we be if in that awful hour we find an advocate in the glorious Archangel Michael! Let us always be faithful in invoking him.

～ *Chapter 3* ～

Veneration of
St. Michael

ACCORDING to the great St. Alphonsus Liguori, veneration of the holy Angels, and particularly of St. Michael, is an outstanding sign of predestination. St. Lawrence Justinian says: "Although we must honor all the Angels, we ought to invoke in a very special manner the glorious St. Michael, as the Prince of all the heavenly spirits, because of his sublime dignity, his pre-eminent office and his invincible power, which he proved in his conflict with Satan, as well as against the combined forces of Hell." Again, the same Saint says: "Let all acknowledge St. Michael as their protector, and be devoted to him, for he cannot despise those who pray to him . . . But he guards them through life, directs them on their way and conducts them to their eternal home."

Holy Church recognizes the exalted dignity and power of St. Michael by the veneration which she pays to him. Until the reform of the breviary in 1961, she had two feasts in his honor—the Apparition of St. Michael on May 8, and the Dedication of St. Michael, or Michaelmas, on September 29. Her liturgy for the latter feast, which she has retained (in the Traditional Latin Mass), is replete with the praises of St. Michael as the Prince of the heavenly hosts and as the protector of the children of God.

Apparition of St. Michael (May 8)

The history of the feast of the Apparition of St. Michael is very remarkable. In the year 492, a wealthy man had a large herd of cattle grazing on Monte Gargano in Italy, not far from the once famous city of Siponto. One day a steer went astray from the herd and did not return with the rest of the cattle at the usual time. The owner and his hired men went in search of the steer and finally found him on the summit of the mountain, lying at the entrance of a cave. The animal refused to leave the spot. At length the owner, exasperated by its stubbornness, took up his bow and sent an arrow toward it. However, the arrow whirled about in the air and, coming directly toward the archer, wounded him.

All were frightened at this strange incident, and no one ventured to approach the place. They went directly to the Bishop of Siponto and related the incident to him. The holy prelate, after serious reflection, decided that there must be some mystery connected with it. He therefore prayed fervently that God's Holy Will might be revealed. Thereupon, St. Michael appeared to him in great splendor and said: "I am Michael the Archangel, who ever stand before the Lord. I am keeping this place under my special protection. By this strange occurrence, I wish to remind men to celebrate the divine service in my honor and that of all the Angels."

After this revelation, the Bishop and all the inhabitants of the place went up the mountain in solemn procession and prayed to the Lord through the intercession of St. Michael. When they arrived at the cave, they found an entrance which led down a stairway. No one, however, ventured to enter, and they performed their devotions at the opening. After that, many pilgrimages were made to this spot.

Much later, around the year 663, the Neapolitans decided to make war upon the inhabitants of Siponto and Benevento. The latter, at the advice of their bishop, kept a three days' fast and called upon the assistance of the holy Archangel. During the night preceding the attack, the Archangel again appeared to the Bishop and told him that God had listened to their petitions and that in the fourth hour of the day they should courageously meet the enemy, and they would gain the victory.

As soon as the attack began, all Monte Gargano was violently shaken. The entire summit was enveloped in dark clouds, from which flashes of lightning, like fiery arrows, flew toward the enemy—who in consequence took to flight. In joy and gratitude and amidst devout prayer, the conquerors entered the sacred spot. They found the cavern to be perfectly formed for a church which could hold about five hundred persons.

This cave had evidently been a place of refuge in which the early Christians had secretly held their services during times of persecution. From a crevice in the rock, which formed the ceiling of this sanctuary, water dripped down upon the rocks. This water was very refreshing and most pleasant to the taste, and it possessed healing properties. Many sick persons were instantly cured after drinking this water; others found health through the intercession of St. Michael. Many other miracles proved this place to be under the special protection of Heaven. Alongside of this subterranean church the bishop erected another, in which the services were conducted by canons regular (priests who belong to a religious order). This church still exists.

The Dedication of St. Michael

The Feast of Saint Michael, or Michaelmas Day, is September 29. As it is not certain just what church is commemorated as having been dedicated on this day, the pious belief has gained favor that the entire Catholic Church is here indicated. For by casting the rebel spirits into the abyss, St. Michael dedicated the Church Triumphant in Heaven as the peaceful abode of the Angels; and as he wards off the devil and his colleagues from the Church upon earth, he has dedicated the Church Militant as the secure dwelling place of the faithful upon earth. Finally, as helper and consoler of the souls in Purgatory, the Church Suffering is placed under his care. This feast of St. Michael has ever been one of the outstanding feasts of the Church. However, the liturgy for the feast is not confined to the veneration of St. Michael alone, but includes all the Angels, particularly those who are appointed as guardians of mankind.

Past and Present Times

The Irish people have always held the captain of the heavenly host in great veneration, as is evident from the number of ancient churches dedicated to him and the frequency with which his name is given to their children. They termed him *"Adrigh na Aaingeal"*—"the High King of the Angels." Veneration of St. Michael was at one time practiced so extensively in England that in the year 1114 King Ethelred ordained that the three days immediately preceding the Feast of St. Michael should be days of strict fast. In the Middle Ages the knights especially consecrated themselves to St. Michael. The German people, too, have long been fervently devoted to this holy Archangel. Devotion to St. Michael is likewise gaining favor in our own country.

∽ *Chapter 4* ∽

Prayers

Mass for the Dedication of St. Michael (September 29)
(In the Traditional Latin Liturgy)

Introit. (*Ps*. 102). Bless the Lord, all ye His angels: you that are mighty in strength, and execute His word, hearkening to the voice of His orders. *Ps*. Bless the Lord, O my soul; and let all that is within me bless His holy Name. *V*. Glory be to the Father . . .

Collect. O God, Who, in a wonderful order, providest ministries both of angels and of men, grant in Thy mercy that they who ever stand before Thy face to minister unto Thee in Heaven may protect us during our life upon earth. Through our Lord . . .

Lesson. (*Apoc*. 1:1-5). In those days: God

signified the things which must shortly come to pass, sending by His angel to His servant John, who hath given testimony to the word of God, and the testimony of Jesus Christ, what things soever he hath seen. Blessed is he that readeth and heareth the words of this prophecy and keepeth those things which are written in it, for the time is at hand. John to the seven churches which are in Asia: Grace be unto you and peace from Him that is, and that was, and that is to come; and from the seven spirits which are before His throne; and from Jesus Christ, who is the faithful witness, the first begotten of the dead, and the prince of the kings of the earth, who hath loved us, and washed us from our sins in His own Blood.

Gradual. Bless the Lord, all ye His angels: you that are mighty in strength, that do His Will. *V.* O my soul, bless thou the Lord: and all that is within me praise His holy name.

Alleluia, alleluia. *V.* Holy Archangel Michael, defend us in battle: that we may not perish in the dreadful judgment. Alleluia.

Instead of the Gradual above, the following is said during Easter time:

Alleluia, alleluia. *V.* Holy Archangel Michael, defend us in battle, that we may not perish in the dreadful judgment. Alleluia. *V.* The sea was shaken and the earth trembled when the Archangel Michael descended from Heaven. Alleluia.

Gospel. (*Matt.* 18:1-10). At that time, the disciples came to Jesus, saying, "Who, thinkest Thou, is the greater in the kingdom of heaven? And Jesus calling unto Him a little child, set him in the midst of them, and said, Amen I say to you, unless you be converted, and become as little children, you shall not enter into the kingdom of heaven. Whosoever, therefore, shall humble himself as this little child, he is the greater in the kingdom of heaven: and he that shall receive one such little child in My name, receiveth Me; but he that shall scandalize one of these little ones that believe in Me, it were better for him that a millstone should be hanged about his neck, and that he should be drowned in the depth of the sea. Woe to the world because of scandals: for it must needs be that scandals come; but nevertheless, woe to that man by whom the scandal cometh. And if thy hand or thy foot scandalize thee, cut it off and cast it from thee. It is better for thee to go into life maimed or lame, than having two hands or two feet, to be cast into everlasting fire. And if thy eye scandalize thee, pluck it out, and cast it from thee. It is better for thee, having one eye, to enter into life, than having two eyes, to be cast into hell fire. See that you despise not one of these little ones; for I say to you, that their angels in heaven always see the face of My Father who is in heaven.

Offertory. (*Apoc.* 8). An angel stood near the altar of the temple, having a golden censer in his hand: and there was given to him much incense: and the smoke of the perfumes ascended before God, Alleluia.

Secret. We offer Thee a sacrifice of praise, O Lord, and humbly beseech Thee that, through the prayers of Thy holy angels who plead for us, Thou wouldst graciously receive it, and grant that it may avail us unto salvation. Through Our Lord . . .

Communion. (*Dan.* 3:58). All ye angels of the Lord, bless the Lord: sing a hymn, and exalt Him above all forever.

Postcommunion. Supported by the intercession of blessed Michael, Thine Archangel, we humbly entreat Thee, O Lord, that the service we pay with our lips, we may lay hold of with our minds. Through Our Lord . . .

* * *

Prayer after Low Mass
(Promulgated by Pope Leo XIII)

ST. MICHAEL the Archangel, defend us in battle; be our defense against the wickedness and snares of the devil. May God rebuke him, we humbly pray; and do thou, O Prince of the heavenly host, by the power of God, cast into Hell Satan and all the other evil spirits, who prowl about the world seeking the ruin of souls. Amen.

For Help against
Spiritual Enemies

O GLORIOUS St. Michael, Prince of the heavenly hosts, who art ever ready to assist the people of God; who fought with the Dragon, the Old Serpent, and cast him out of heaven, and now dost valiantly defend the Church of God so that the gates of Hell may never prevail against her: I earnestly entreat thee to assist me also in the painful and dangerous conflict I must sustain against the same formidable foe. Be with me, O Mighty Prince! that I may courageously fight and wholly vanquish that proud spirit whom thou, by the divine power, have overthrown, and whom our powerful King, Jesus Christ, in our nature so completely overcame; so that, triumphing over the enemy of my salvation, I may, with thee and the holy Angels, praise the clemency of God, who, though refusing mercy to the rebellious angels after their fall, has granted repentance and forgiveness to fallen man. Amen.

Prayer for Perseverance

O GOD, Who made blessed Michael, Thine Archangel, victorious over the proud Lucifer and all the wicked spirits, we beseech Thee that, fighting under the Cross and ever adopting his maxim, "Who is like unto God," we may be victorious over all our enemies and be delivered from all evils. Do Thou regulate our lives according to Thy Will and Commandments. Through Jesus Christ our Lord. Amen.

For Assistance at the Hour of Death

O GLORIOUS Archangel St. Michael, by thy protection, enable my soul to be so enriched by grace as to be worthy to be presented by thee to Jesus Christ, my Judge, at the hour of my death. As thou didst conquer Satan and expel him from heaven, conquer him again and drive him far away from me at the hour of my death. Amen.

O Mary, Queen of Heaven, procure for me the assistance of St. Michael at the hour of my death!

For the Reign
Of the Sacred Heart

O MARY IMMACULATE, great Queen of Heaven and earth and our gentle advocate, deign, we beseech thee, to intercede for us. Ask God to send St. Michael and the holy Angels to ward off all the obstacles contrary to the reign of the Sacred Heart in our souls, our families, our country, and in the whole world.

And thou, O holy Michael, Prince of the Heavenly Hosts, from our hearts we beg thee to come to our aid.

Defend us against the rage of Satan, and through the divine power bestowed upon thee by God, after securing victory for the Church here below, guide our souls to our eternal home. Amen.

St. Michael, First Champion of the Kingship of Christ, pray for us!

Novena to St. Michael

A novena (prayer prayed every day for nine days) may be made at any time of the year, with any approved prayers.

Prayer to St. Michael

O GLORIOUS Prince of the heavenly hosts and victor over rebellious spirits, be mindful of me who am so weak and sinful and yet so prone to pride and ambition. Lend me, I pray, thy powerful aid in every temptation and difficulty, and above all do not forsake me in my last struggle with the powers of evil. Amen.

The Angelic Trisagion

H OLY, Holy, Holy, Lord God of Hosts, the heavens and the earth are full of Thy glory.

St. Michael, the Archangel, defend us in the battle, that we may not perish in the dreadful judgment. Amen.

Prayer for Protection of the Church and Her Members

O GLORIOUS St. Michael, Guardian and Defender of the Church of Jesus Christ, come to the assistance of the Church, against which the powers of Hell are unchained. Guard with thy special care her august visible head, and obtain for him and for us that the hour of triumph may speedily arrive. O glorious Archangel St. Michael, watch over us during life, defend us against the assaults of the demon, assist us especially at the hour of death, obtain for us a favorable judgment and the happiness of beholding God face to face for endless ages. Amen.

The Angelic Crown or Chaplet
(Chaplet of St. Michael the Archangel)

On the medal:
V. O God, come to my assistance.
R. O Lord, make haste to help me.
Glory be to the Father . . .

Before each salutation, recite one *Our Father* on the individual bead and three *Hail Marys* on the three beads grouped together, in honor of the corresponding Choir of Angels. (Leave the set of four beads until the end. See p. 53.)

First Salutation. At the intercession of St. Michael and the heavenly choir of the *Seraphim*, may it please God to make us worthy to receive into our hearts the fire of His perfect charity. Amen.

Second Salutation. At the intercession of St. Michael and the heavenly choir of the *Cherubim*, may God grant us the grace to abandon the ways of sin and follow the path of Christian perfection. Amen.

Third Salutation. At the intercession of St. Michael and the heavenly choir of the *Thrones*, may it please God to infuse into our hearts a true and earnest spirit of humility. Amen.

Fourth Salutation. At the intercession of St. Michael and the heavenly choir of the *Dominations*, may it please God to grant us the grace to have dominion over our senses and to correct our depraved passions. Amen.

Fifth Salutation. At the intercession of St. Michael and the heavenly choir of the *Powers*, may God vouchsafe to keep our souls from the wiles and temptations of the devil. Amen.

Sixth Salutation. At the intercession of St. Michael and the choir of the admirable celestial *Virtues*, may Our Lord keep us from falling into temptations and deliver us from evil. Amen.

Seventh Salutation. At the intercession of St. Michael and the heavenly choir of the *Principalities*, may it please God to fill our hearts with the spirit of true and hearty obedience. Amen.

Eighth Salutation. At the intercession of St. Michael and the heavenly choir of *Archangels*, may it please God to grant us the gift of perseverance in the Faith and in all good works, that we may thereby be enabled to attain unto the glory of Paradise. Amen.

Ninth Salutation. At the intercession of St. Michael and the heavenly choir of holy *Angels*, may God vouchsafe to grant that they may protect us during life, and after death may lead us into the everlasting glory of Heaven. Amen.

Then say the *Our Father* on each of the four remaining beads: the first in honor of St. Michael, the second in honor of St. Gabriel, the third in honor of St. Raphael, and the fourth in honor of your Guardian Angel. End as follows:

St. Michael, glorious Prince, Chief and Champion of the Heavenly Host, guardian of the souls of men, conqueror of the rebel angels, steward of the palace of God under Jesus Christ, our worthy leader, endowed with superhuman excellence and virtue: free us from every ill, who with full confidence have recourse to thee; and by thine incomparable protection, enable us to make progress every day in the faithful service of our God. Amen.

V. Pray for us, most blessed Michael, Prince of the Church of Jesus Christ.
R. That we may be made worthy of His promises.

Let us pray.

Almighty and eternal God, Who in Thine own marvelous goodness and pity didst, for the common salvation of men, choose the

glorious Archangel Michael to be the Prince
of Thy Church, make us worthy, we pray
Thee, to be delivered by his beneficent protection from all our enemies, that at the
hour of our death, none of them may
approach to harm us; rather, grant that by
the same Archangel Michael we may be
introduced into the presence of Thy Most
High and Divine Majesty. Through the mer-
its of the same Jesus Christ Our Lord.
Amen.

Litany of St. Michael

(For private use.)

Lord, have mercy on us.
  Christ, have mercy on us.
Lord, have mercy on us. Christ, hear us.
  Christ, graciously hear us.
God the Father of Heaven,
  Have mercy on us.
God the Son, Redeemer of the world,
  Have mercy on us.
God the Holy Spirit,
  Have mercy on us.
Holy Trinity, One God,
  Have mercy on us.

Holy Mary, Queen of Angels, *pray for us.*

St. Michael, *pray for us.*

St. Michael, filled with the wisdom of God, *etc.*

St. Michael, perfect adorer of the Incarnate Word,

St. Michael, crowned with honor and glory,

St. Michael, most powerful Prince of the armies of the Lord,

St. Michael, standard-bearer of the Most Holy Trinity,

St. Michael, victor over Satan,

St. Michael, guardian of Paradise,

St. Michael, guide and comforter of the people of Israel,

St. Michael, splendor and fortress of the Church Militant,

St. Michael, honor and joy of the Church Triumphant,

St. Michael, light of angels,

St. Michael, bulwark of orthodox believers,

St. Michael, strength of those who fight under the standard of the Cross,

St. Michael, light and confidence of souls at the hour of death,

St. Michael, our most sure aid,

St. Michael, our help in all adversities,

St. Michael, herald of the everlasting sentence,

St. Michael, consoler of souls detained in the flames of Purgatory,

St. Michael, whom the Lord hath charged to receive souls after death,

St. Michael, our prince.

St. Michael, our advocate,

Lamb of God, Who takest away the sins of the world,
Spare us, O Lord.

Lamb of God, Who takest away the sins of the world,
Graciously hear us, O Lord.

Lamb of God, Who takest away the sins of the world,
Have mercy on us.

Christ, hear us.
Christ, graciously hear us.

V. Pray for us, O glorious St. Michael, Prince of the Church of Jesus Christ,

R. *That we may be made worthy of His promises.*

Let us pray.

Sanctify us, we beseech Thee, O Lord Jesus, with Thy holy blessing, and grant us, by the intercession of St. Michael, that wisdom which teaches us to lay up treasures in Heaven by exchanging the goods of this world for those of eternity, Thou Who livest and reignest, world without end. *Amen.*

Prayer for the Church And for Souls

Recommended for frequent recitation in the present critical times

O GLORIOUS Prince of the heavenly host, St. Michael the Archangel, defend us in the battle and in the fearful warfare we are waging against the principalities and powers, against the rulers of this world of darkness, against the evil spirits. Come thou to the assistance of men, whom Almighty God created immortal, making them in His own image and likeness and redeeming them at a great price from the tyranny of Satan. Fight this day the battle of the Lord with thy legions of holy Angels, even as of old thou didst fight against Lucifer, the leader of the proud spirits and all his rebels angels, who were powerless to stand against thee, neither was their place found any more in heaven. And that apostate angel, transformed into an angel of darkness who still prowls about the earth to encompass our ruin, was cast headlong into the abyss together with his followers. But behold, that first enemy of mankind, a murderer from the beginning, has regained his confidence. Changing himself into "an angel of light," he goes about with the whole multitude of wicked spirits to invade the earth and to blot out the Name of God and of His Christ, to plunder, to slay and to consign to eternal damnation the souls that have been destined for a crown of everlasting life. This wicked serpent, like an unclean torrent, pours into men of depraved minds and corrupt hearts the poison of his malice, the spirit of lying, impiety and blasphemy, and the deadly breath of impurity and every form of vice and iniquity. These crafty enemies of mankind have filled to overflowing with gall and wormwood the Church, which is the Bride of the Lamb without spot; they have laid profane hands upon her most sacred treasures. Make haste, therefore, O invincible Prince, to help the People of God against the inroads of the lost spirits, and grant us the victory. Amen.

Our Father

OUR FATHER, Who art in Heaven, hallowed be Thy Name. Thy kingdom come, Thy will be done, on earth as it is in Heaven. * Give us this day our daily bread, and forgive us our trespasses, as we forgive those who trespass against us. And lead us not into temptation, but deliver us from evil. Amen.

Hail Mary

HAIL MARY, full of grace, the Lord is with thee; blessed art thou among women, and blessed is the Fruit of thy womb, Jesus. * Holy Mary, Mother of God, pray for us sinners, now and at the hour of our death. Amen.

Glory Be

GLORY BE to the Father, and to the Son, and to the Holy Ghost. * As it was in the beginning, is now, and ever shall be, world without end. Amen.

If you have enjoyed this book, consider making your next selection from among the following . . .

Padre Pio and America. *Rega* 18.50
Whole World Will Love Me. *Scallan* 18.50
Tradition and the Church. *Agius* 18.50
Dressing with Dignity. *Hammond* 10.00
Religious Vocation—Unneces. Mystery. *Butler* 12.50
Visits to the Blessed Sacrament. *Liguori* 5.00
The Holy Eucharist—Our All. 3.00
Angels and Devils. *Joan Carroll Cruz* 16.50
Story of a Soul. *St. Therese* 9.00
The Forgotten Secret of Fatima. 2.50
Characters of the Inquisition. *Walsh* 16.50
The Shroud of Turin. *Guerrera* 15.00
St. Catherine Labouré. *Dirvin* 16.50
St. Teresa of Avila. *Walsh* 24.00
Therese Neumann—Mystic and Stigmatist. *Vogl* . . 16.50
Life of the Blessed Virgin Mary. *Emmerich* . . . 18.00
Light and Peace. *Quadrupani*. 8.00
Where We Got the Bible. *Graham* 8.00
Trustful Surrender to Divine Providence 7.00
Charity for the Suffering Souls. *Nageleisen* . . . 18.00
The Voice of the Saints. (Sayings of). 8.00
The Devil—Does He Exist? *Delaporte* 8.50
A Catechism of Modernism. *Lemius* 7.50
St. Bernadette Soubirous. *Trochu* 21.00
The Love of Mary. *Roberto* 9.00
The 12 Steps to Holiness and Salvation. *Liguori* . 9.00
The Rosary and the Crisis of Faith 2.00
Child's Bible History. *Knecht* 7.00
Eucharistic Miracles. *Cruz* 16.50
The Blessed Virgin Mary. *St. Alphonsus* 7.50
Priest, the Man of God. *Cafasso* 16.00

Prices subject to change.

Gift of Oneself. *Schryvers*. 14.00
Humility of Heart. *da Bergamo* 10.00
Mystery of Love for/Single. *Unger* 14.00
Divine Intimacy. Leather. *Fr. Gabriel* 48.00
Great Magdalens. *Blunt*. 18.50
Soul of the Apostolate. *Chautard*. 12.50
Little Catechism of the Curé of Ars. *Vianney*. . 8.00
The Four Last Things. *von Cochem* 9.00
The Cure of Ars. *O'Brien* 7.50
The Angels—Cath. Teaching. *Parente* 12.00
Moments Divine—Before Bl. Sacrament *Reuter*. . 10.00
Saints Who Raised/Dead—400 Miracles 18.50
Wonder of Guadalupe. *Johnston*. 9.00
St. Gertrude the Great 2.50
Mystical City of God. (abr.) *Agreda* 21.00
Sermons of the Curé of Ars. *Vianney* 15.00
Who Is Padre Pio? *Radio Replies Press* 3.00
What Will Hell Be Like? *St. Alphonsus* 1.50
Life and Glories of St. Joseph. *Thompson* 16.50
The Curé D'Ars. *Abbé Francis Trochu* 24.00
What Catholics Believe. *Lovasik* 6.00
Clean Love in Courtship. *Lovasik* 4.50
Self-Abandonment to Div. Prov. *de Caussade* . 22.50
Canons & Decrees of the Council of Trent. . . . 16.50
Love, Peace and Joy. *St. Gertrude/Prévot* 8.00
St. Joseph Cafasso—Priest of Gallows. *St. J. Bosco* . 6.00
Mother of God/Her Glorious Feasts. *O'Laverty* . 15.00
Apologetics. *Glenn*. 12.50
Isabella of Spain. *William Thomas Walsh* 24.00
Philip II. H.B. *Walsh*. (Reg. 45.00) 30.00
Fundamentals of Catholic Dogma. *Ott* 27.50
Creation Rediscovered. *Keane* 21.00
Hidden Treasure—Holy Mass. *St. Leonard* 7.50
St. Philomena. *Mohr* 12.00
Prices subject to change.

St. Michael the Archangel 3.00
Joy in Suffering/St. Therese. *Noser* 3.50
Your Labor of Love. *Penny*............... 12.00
Your Vocation of Love. *Penny*............. 14.00
Set of 2 Above (Reg. 26.00) 20.00
Thirty Favorite Novenas.................... 1.50
Devotion to Infant Jesus of Prague 1.50
On Freemasonry *(Humanum Genus). Leo XIII* . 2.50
Thoughts of the Curé D'Ars. *St. John Vianney* 3.00
Way of the Cross. *St. Alphonsus Liguori* 1.50
Way of the Cross. *Franciscan*............... 1.50
Magnificent Prayers. *St. Bridget of Sweden* ... 2.00
Douay-Rheims New Testament 16.50
Life of Christ. 4 vols. P.B. *Emmerich.* (Reg. 75.00) . 60.00
The Ways of Mental Prayer. *Lehodey* 16.50
Miraculous Images of Our Lord. *Cruz* 16.50
Bl. Jacinta Marto of Fatima. *Cirrincione* 3.00
Bl. Francisco Marto of Fatima. *Cirrincione,* comp... 2.50
Is It a Saint's Name? *Dunne*................. 3.00
Prophets and Our Times. *Culleton* 15.00
Purgatory and Heaven. *Arendzen* 6.00
Rosary in Action. *Johnson* 12.00
Sacred Heart and the Priesthood. *de la Touche* 10.00
Story of the Church. *Johnson et al* 22.50
Latin Grammar. *Scanlon & Scanlon* 18.00
Second Latin. *Scanlon & Scanlon* 16.50
Christ Denied. *Wickens* 3.50
Agony of Jesus. *Padre Pio* 3.00
Tour of the Summa. *Glenn* 22.50
Three Conversions/Spir. Life. *Garrigou-Lagrange* 7.00
The Sinner's Guide. *Ven. Louis of Granada* ... 15.00
Radio Replies. 3 Vols. *Rumble & Carty* 48.00
Rhine Flows into the Tiber. *Wiltgen*.......... 16.50
Sermons on Prayer. *St. Francis de Sales*...... 7.00

Prices subject to change.